NATION BUILDING

FOR WOMEN

what you need to know

before entering a

polygynous marriage

Shanelle Shalom

Nation Building: What You Need To Know Before Entering A Polygynous Marriage
Written by Shanelle Shalom
Queens of Marriage Prep & Femininity Coaching
November 2020
Bible verses taken from *The Holy Bible King James Version Large Print Compact Edition* © Copyright 2000

Introduction

Polygamy is, and may always be, a controversial topic among men and women of western society. Though it is still practiced in other cultures around the world, *polygyny* (the form of polygamy in which a man has more than one wife) is viewed as an ancient, outdated marital arrangement that is no longer needed, or no longer *accepted*, in today's society. Most western women are not fond of the idea of husband sharing, even when they claim to believe in "sisterhood". It appears as if women are only willing to share minor resources and emotional support with other women, but not willing to share the most significant resource a woman can have—a husband—with their "sisters".

Truth be told, women have always shared men, whether voluntarily or involuntarily. Of course, not every single woman on earth had to share her husband, but the sharing of men has always went on—even now. Some women have agreed to open relationships, others have agreed to polygyny, and many others were subject to infidelity. Nonetheless, all of these women shared their husband with another woman, whether they wanted to or not. But had it not been for *infidelity*, it is possible that women's distaste for polygyny wouldn't be as strong. When you are used to seeing men sneaking and deceiving their way into the arms of another woman, it is no wonder you want to stay far away from anything that reminds you of it.

If you feel that infidelity and polygyny are two sides of the same coin, then it's time for you to get a thorough education of what polygyny is really about...and you've come to the right place! *Nation Building For Women* was written to educate you about polygyny so that you can make an educated decision about if the arrangement is right for you. If it is, you will have the knowledge needed to proceed in a safe, orderly manner. Please understand that this book was not written to convince you to be in a polygynous marriage. I understand that polygyny is not for everyone. Everyone cannot do it, nor does everyone want to, and that's okay.

After reading *Nation Building For Women*, you may decide that you do not want to be in a polygynous marriage, but I am confident that your respect for the practice will be greatly increased. That alone, is a victory! Much of the ill feelings women have toward polygyny is due to misunderstanding the purpose and intentions behind it. They believe it is practically the same as infidelity. So, before we get started, I want to make it clear that polygyny and infidelity are not the same. **In polygyny, (1) everyone has consented, (2) the women involved know about each other, and (3) the man *marries* each woman.** If all the women haven't consented or they do not know about each other, then it *is* infidelity. And if the man is sleeping with them without marrying them, then it is *polyamory*—not polygyny. Polygyny is *marriage*.

Now that we got that out of the way, let's dive deeper into the world of polygyny, shall we? Hold on to your seats...

NATION BUILDING FOR WOMEN

CHAPTER 1

Laying the Foundation

Biblical Polygyny

Interestingly enough, there actually aren't many scriptures in the bible about how a polygynous marriage should operate. We definitely see examples of polygyny being practiced, but we don't see much instruction on how to or how *not* to do it. Unfortunately, this has caused a little confusion among communities where polygyny is embraced, because there are so many details left up for debate. Now, polygynous men are left to make up their own rules, and the women don't have a template on how to enter the arrangement with confidence that they will be respected and protected. With no clear standard on how to do polygyny, women *and men* are put at the mercy of people who have ulterior motives. How do we solve this problem?

We will take the polygyny stories that are given to us in the bible and use them to our benefit. There are valuable lessons to be learned from them, and even more to be learned from other biblical principles throughout the bible. The bible technically has all the information we need to have an orderly polygynous marriage. Of course, it will be a little more complicated than a regular marriage. Nonetheless, it is still just a marriage, and there are plenty of scriptures on that.

A Fruitful Marriage

A major reason why some women don't understand the purpose of a polygynous marriage is because they don't quite grasp the purpose of marriage *in general*. We've been taught that marriage is for two people who are in love, coming together to share their love for the remainder of their lives. Loving your partner is important, but that should not be the only motivation to get married. Let's take a moment to sum up the true purpose (and benefits) of marriage in the points below...

1. **Marriage builds a nation.** Biblically, nations were formed from the descendants of a man. Some nations were considered righteous and blessed, while others were wicked and cursed. This could possibly be the most important reason why women should be careful about the man they choose to have children with. If a man isn't in God's favor, marrying him and having his children puts this cursed man as the head of your family, causing the whole family (or nation) to suffer from the judgment that will come upon him for his wrongdoings. Deuteronomy 5:9-10 says, *"For I the Lord thy God am a jealous God, visiting the iniquity of the fathers upon the children, unto the third and fourth generation of those that hate me. And showing mercy unto thousands of them who love me and keep my commandments."* The sins *or* the obedience of the father can affect the whole nation, so please choose the father of your nation wisely.

2. **Marriage expands a nation.** Marriage allows you and your husband to expand and extend your bloodline. Have you ever noticed that the righteous are not being fruitful and multiplying nearly as fast as the unrighteous? Take

a look around you. The women and men who are dysfunctional and wicked are having multiple children, oftentimes with multiple people, while the righteous either have no children or only a fraction of the children the unrighteous have. The righteous tend to have children later in life, past their prime, and only procreate with one person. This puts the functional people at a disadvantage in society because they are being out-produced by the dysfunctional. Instead of extending their bloodline, they are restraining it, and suffering from the consequences of being outnumbered by people who are much less lawful and orderly than they are. How can we build a righteous nation if the righteous folks fail to reproduce?

3. **Marriage gives the nation an identity.** Identity is something that many fatherless children have been robbed of, which is why many of them go out into the world seeking an identity elsewhere. They look to their peers, people in the streets, entertainers, even strangers on social media for ideas on who they should or shouldn't be. They are like a lost puppy who can't find their home, all because their fathers were never there to give them a sense of direction and belonging. But when children are born within marriage, they benefit from receiving a sense of identity from their father, as he teaches them who they are, what values and principles the family represents, and what they are expected to live up to. The children can then walk around with confidence, having purpose, direction and identity until they are old enough to go off and create their own nation.

4. **Marriage transfers power and resources.** It is honorable to be charitable and share your wealth with the less fortunate, but you are to keep the bulk of your wealth in your own family. Marriage makes it possible for you to transfer wealth to your spouse and offspring, especially in the event of death. But your family won't only inherit physical wealth, they'll inherit your position, too. Let's say you are the CEO of your own business. You can leave your position to your spouse or child once you are disabled or deceased. Spiritual inheritances like favor, honor and wisdom can be passed to your family, as

well. Simply put, marriage allows us to inherit *privilege*—something that many families could desperately use. When children come from a family where there is no inheritance, they are left to build their own identity and wealth from scratch, which puts them at a disadvantage in a world where other children come from families that give them a leg up.

5. **Marriage creates a high quality of life.** The structure, security and status that comes from a healthy marriage cannot be duplicated in any other kind of relationship, but we don't think much of marriage anymore because many marriages are below standard. For example, married couples today are shortsighted. Couples focus more on their own needs, failing to plan for the needs of their offspring. Others plan for their children, but don't think about their grandchildren. All these things were considered back in biblical times. When you are thinking of the wellbeing and livelihood of grandchildren, great grandchildren and so forth, it will allow you to form a plan on how you're going to create a respectable family name and reputation that brings honor to *all* your family—not just the ones who happen to living under your roof at the given moment.

Now that you see the benefits of marriage, you can probably start to understand why some people prefer to establish a polygynous marriage in order to multiply the benefits. Once we decide that we want to marry, whether in monogamy or polygyny, we should come to the table ready to discuss what's in it for both or all parties involved. Clear expectations need to be set, or else someone could enter the marriage getting more (or less) than they bargained for.

Settling For Single

The benefits listed in "A Fruitful Marriage" are very difficult to acquire as a single woman. Single women work very hard each day, trying to accumulate their own wealth, status, happiness, and fulfillment, but doing so without a partner. They don't admit how hard it is to do it all alone, nor how exhausted they feel at the end of each day. On top of that, some of them have children they are raising alone. They don't have the emotional, financial or spiritual support they truly need, but put on a brave face and say they are happy being single and don't need a husband. I understand that some women really are okay with being single, and if you are one of them, then you have every right to not marry if you feel that is best. But before you settle for single, please seriously ask yourself if being single is better than having a reliable, lifelong partner. Living as a single woman can be comfortable for a certain period of time, but after a while, it can get challenging.

1. If you settle for singlehood, you will be settling for periods of **loneliness.** Sometimes we have people around us, but still feel lonely due to the lack of companionship and intimacy. Not having someone to share your deepest thoughts and ideas with, someone to show you affection or to engage in hobbies with can make any sane person feel lonely. Humans *need* relationships. We need to experience love and intimacy on many levels, and in many ways.

2. Singlehood can also result in **promiscuity**. Whenever there is a need for sexual intimacy, instead of engaging in it with their husband, single women are doing it with multiple men—men who probably have no interest in loving them, providing for them, protecting them, nor committing to them. It's risky behavior, but because it's so common, women no longer view it as risky until consequences arise.

3. Being single can leave you with very little to **no protection.** There is a sense of safety and security that women feel when they have a trustworthy man that will do whatever he can to keep her out of harm's way, whether it be physically, emotionally or spiritually. Protection is something all women need and crave. It's a priceless gift that men give the special woman (or women) in their life.

4. Single women suffer from a **lack of guidance**. They are left to their own devices, having to figure things out for themselves, without the input of someone who is invested in their success. Of course, you can make good decisions on your own, but it is a known fact that men have a different way of thinking and reasoning than women do. When we don't have the option of benefiting from the male perspective, the choices we make may not be as good had we had someone to help guide us in our decision making.

5. Singleness usually leads to a **lack of wealth.** Think about how much more you would have if someone helped you build wealth. Think about what your children and grandchildren would inherit. The truth is, there aren't many single women leaving behind thousands of dollars, homes and land for their children to inherit. Children that come from single mother households usually have to build their own wealth from scratch because their mothers couldn't afford to give them a financial jumpstart.

While some women act proud to be single, we're going to be *honest* about what singlehood really entails: It's not all girls' trips, parties and bubble baths. Tears, exhaustion, disappointment and loneliness comes with it, too. That's the ugly side that no one wants to talk about, but marriage to the right man fixes these things. We know that finding a good man isn't easy, and finding one that is truly monogamous makes it even harder. I say this because there are plenty of women who are in what appears to be a monogamous relationship, but behind the scenes, their husband has a mistress. He may love his wife dearly, maybe even been married to her several years, but over those years, he had a couple of girlfriends outside the marriage. This is very common. We have self-proclaimed monogamous men who are not completely monogamous. They may not want more than one *wife*, but they do want more than one *woman*.

This isn't acceptable for every woman, so some have decided that if they can't have a monogamous husband then they don't want a husband at all. That is perfectly fine, but does remaining single mean that they won't be with a man at all, or does it mean they just won't get married? If you share the same sentiments as these women, keep in mind that you cannot be single *and* have sex with men who aren't your husband and still be a righteous woman. Are you willing to be abstinent while single? If not, then you should marry. 1 Corinthians 7:8-9 says, *"I say therefore to the unmarried and widows, it is good for them if they abide even as I (single and abstinent), but if they cannot contain, let them marry, for it is better to marry than to burn."* Don't opt for the single life if you aren't willing and ready to live single the righteous way.

According to scripture, in the last days, single women will desperately try to find a husband, so much so that they will actually propose marriage. Not a monogamous marriage, but a polygynous marriage! Isaiah 3:25-4:1 says, *"Thy men shall fall by the sword, and thy mighty in the war. And her gates shall lament and mourn; and she being desolate shall sit upon the ground. And in that day, seven women shall take hold of one man, saying, "We will eat our own bread, and wear our own apparel. Only let us be called by thy name to take away our reproach."* As you can see, a shortage of men will force women to take desperate measures that they may not have taken under other circumstances. Right now, there are already women who are feeling the sting of a man shortage, and have already begun clamoring for the few available men that are left.

The fact that these women are saying *"We will eat our own bread and wear our own apparel"* sounds as if they are the "independent women" we know today. They say they don't need a man to take care of them, and then there are those who say they will never marry a polygynous man unless he is wealthy enough to take care of all his wives. But when push comes to shove, they both will have to take care of themselves *while* being in a polygynous marriage. It's clear that these women will not search for a husband for guidance, protection and provision, but so they can avoid the shame of being single. Again, there is no shame in being single if you do so righteously. If you later decide to marry, a man will gladly cover you. But the unrighteous single women will be the ones desperately begging for a husband.

I pray that you are blessed enough to marry and enjoy the fruits of marriage, no matter if the marriage is polygynous or monogamous. If you feel that a monogamous marriage is the best option for you, be realistic about what it will require of you in this day and age. If you want a husband who is going to be faithful to just one woman for the rest of his life, then you will have to be a standout woman. Proverbs 31:10 says, *"Who can find a virtuous woman? For her price is far above rubies."* If that question was asked back in a time where virtuous women were more plentiful, imagine how hard it is to find one now. You will have to be one of those hard-to-find virtuous women. That means being all that God requires of you.

NATION BUILDING
FOR WOMEN

CHAPTER 2
Poly Problems

Polygyny vs. Polyandry vs. Monogamy

A huge concern that women have about polygyny is that the husband will benefit from it more than the wives. They think the #1 benefit would be an abundance of sex, which isn't a bad thing, but apparently it's perceived to be. Monogamy ensures that men don't get this benefit. A monogamous man only gets as much sex as his only wife allows. If his wife withholds sex from him, he'll just have to suffer it out, but a polygynist has the option of going to his other wife for sex. Most western women do not want their husband to be able to do this, especially if they cannot do the same.

Let's say we decided to marry multiple men, for argument's sake. We would not get the same results as a man who practices polygyny. Multiple husbands (*polyandry*) defeat the whole purpose of nation building. We can only get pregnant by one husband at a time, which is no different than when we have only *one* husband. On top of that, we wouldn't know which husband fathered the child, being that we were sleeping with all of them. A woman can only produce one man's seed at a time, no matter how many men she's sleeping with. But a man who has three wives will be able to produce three children at one time. That is a privilege of nation building that is only awarded to polygynists.

A polyandrous woman is not building her family any faster than a woman who has one husband. The only benefit she could get from having multiple husbands is *financial*. Multiple men working and providing for one woman can give her and their children a wealthy lifestyle, which sounds great. But the chances of a woman finding multiple men who are willing to provide for her *and* share her sexually with other men is very slim—much slimmer than it is for a man to find multiple *women* who would share *him*. Men who are dominant in nature will not participate in polyandry because they are territorial and protective. If you manage to find a man who will share you with other men, they will likely have a submissive, effeminate personality. These men do not make good leaders or protectors. Any man who allows another man to sleep with his wife is hardly protective.

It's important that we compare polygyny and polyandry because you need to know that if you were to have a polygynous marriage, the results would not be the same. There is no need to believe that men only practice polygyny for selfish reasons, because if *you* were to practice it, nature will yield you unfavorable results regardless of your reasons, and nature will yield men *better* results regardless of *their* reasons. You can argue whether or not men should practice polygyny, but you cannot argue with nature. I'm only putting this out there for the women who believe that there is a double standard when it comes to the practice of polygamy. Some double standards are ingrained in nature, and there is nothing anyone can do to change that—not even you.

There are more polygynous men among us than we think, but many of them claim to be monogamous because they aren't allowed to claim anything else. This is why they end up sneaking around with other women. We created a culture where men cannot come out and say they want more than one woman and still be considered a good man. To us, a good man must be *monogamous*. Until we change that idea, men will continue to hide who they are, and we will continue to find out who they *really* are the hard way.

Anti-Polygyny Arguments Debunked

There are a few common misconceptions about polygyny that desperately need to be addressed. There could be women reading this that are capable of being in a polygynous relationship, but are being led away by misguided opinions of other people. Let's take some time to address these misconceptions and give clarity and solutions to them...

Misconception #1: Polygyny is all about sex. If you believe men want multiple wives only for sex, then you may also subconsciously believe that sex is all women have to offer. If a woman is being the kind of wife she was created to be—a helper and supporter of her husband, a keeper of her household, and a multiplier of his wealth, then why *wouldn't* a man want more than one? Now, there are some men who want to be polygynous because they desire to engage in threesomes, so if you are considering being with a polygynous man, be sure that sexual fetishes are not his main motivation for marrying you. Ask him early on why he wants to be in a polygynous marriage. Pay attention to his reasoning and see if it makes any sense to you. If you feel that his intentions are impure, then follow your gut and decline.

Misconception #2: Men can't do right by one wife, let alone two. It's true that a lot of men have failed in monogamous relationships, but many women have, as well. Just as the men could not do right by one woman, the women could not do right by their man. They have been with multiple men in their lifetime, but failed to *keep* any of them. Yet they are saying men cannot do right by one woman, as if they've done a great job with men. No matter what kind of relationship a man is in, monogamous or polygynous, if he is not dealing with cooperative, supportive women, then he is not going to have much success. If it is necessary to point out that men haven't done well with monogamy, then we must also acknowledge that we are partially responsible for their failure. A polygynous man who manages to find cooperative women who are willing to work with him will have more success than a monogamous man who has to deal with an uncooperative woman.

Misconception #3: It's unsanitary. This is a non-issue. A man and his wives can easily get each other tested before they engage in sexual activity. That would be the responsible thing to do whether you are polygynous or not. People don't enter marriages as virgins anymore, so who knows what diseases or infections they could have picked up along the way. The sensible thing to do would be to get tested. For some reason, we have this idea that serial monogamy—dating/having sex with one person, then moving on to another, and then to another and so on—is clean just because we are having sex with one partner at a time. But serial monogamy is not sanitary. It's a shame that we think sharing our bodies with several people who've also shared their bodies with several people is more sanitary than a man *committing* to the same partners.

Misconception #4: Most men can't afford it. It's true that most men can't afford to take care of multiple wives, but most men aren't trying to be polygynists either. For some reason, we assume that the few men who *do* want to be polygynous cannot afford it, as if we know what their bank account looks like. Like I mentioned earlier, if a polygynous man finds women who are willing to work with him, he can get way more accomplished with them than he ever did with women who are stubborn and unsupportive. They can put their heads together, pool their resources and create ideas to generate wealth. Make no mistake about it, money can be made as long as they are willing to help each other. How much money they have going into it doesn't really determine anything. It's all about how much money they will generate *together*.

Misconception #5: Women who agree to polygyny are desperate. Every woman who's in a polygynous marriage can definitely have a man to herself if she wanted to, but what kind of man would it be? Would it be a righteous man? Would it be a man of quality? Some women would rather share a great man than to have a mediocre man to themselves. As satisfying to your ego as it may be to have a man to yourself, you may be sacrificing quality in exchange for exclusivity. There are way too many women who are in relationships with men who do not treat them well, but they put up with it just because he's not cheating. Women who share a husband have different priorities. They prefer upstanding men who offer them something they cannot get from just any man. They also want the benefits of having a reliable sisterhood, and some recognize that there are not enough good men for all of us to have one to ourselves. This is a reality that some women have faced that others are still in denial about. Once we all understand that other women are in need of a decent husband just like we are, then maybe we will understand why sharing is necessary in some cases.

Misconception #6: Polygyny is a sin. The bible says sin is transgression of the law (1 John 3:4). There is no law against polygyny, which means polygyny is not a transgression of the law, therefore polygyny is not a sin. If it is something you don't want to practice, then that is 100% okay, but you don't have to say that polygyny is a sin to make yourself feel justified for being against it. It can be lawful, yet still something you don't want for yourself. Just don't treat the people who do practice it as if they are doing something unlawful, because they are not.

Misconception #7: Polygyny is being forced on women. Much of the media that you come across where people are discussing polygyny are only recognizing that there is an alternative to monogamy and giving you information on its benefits. There is no force, but if you feel it's being forced on women, then you now know how men feel when monogamy was forced on them for all these years.

Favoritism & Jealousy

We can't talk about polygyny without talking about *favoritism & jealousy*! They both are a reality of polygyny that we tend not to properly address. Maybe it makes us uncomfortable because it exposes our weak areas. Favoritism exposes the weakness of the husband and jealousy exposes the weakness of the wives. But we see in scripture that favoritism and jealousy did occur in polygynous marriages. Favoritism is addressed in Deuteronomy 21:15-16, which says, *"If a man has two wives, one loved and the other hated, and they have born him children (both the loved and the hated), and if the first born son is of her who is hated, then it shall be when he maketh his sons to inherit that which he has, that he may not make the son of the loved as firstborn before the son of the hated, which is indeed the firstborn."* What the scripture is saying is that a man should not give an inheritance that belongs to the son of the wife he *doesn't* favor, to the son of the wife he *does*. The husband should do what is just and give the rightful son his inheritance regardless of how he feels about his mother.

Polygynous men would definitely show extreme levels of favoritism if God didn't make it a law not to. And even though it is a law, some still show favoritism in other ways. So, how can this be prevented? Or can it be prevented at all? Can a man really love all his wives *equally*? The truth is, a man can have the discipline to not openly display favoritism, but he still may have a favorite wife. There is nothing anyone can do to stop him from feeling more love for one wife over the other. That is why God made it a law that the husband *does* what is fair, not *feels* what is fair. Notice that the scripture doesn't tell the man that he has to feel the same for both wives, but that he has to *do right* by both wives.

It's important to make a distinction between emotional love and dutiful love because they are not the same. Exodus 21:10-11 says, *"If he takes another wife, "he shall not diminish her food, clothing and marital rights. If he does not do these three for her, then she shall go out free, without paying money."* This is dutiful love, not emotional love. A husband has certain responsibilities to his wives regardless of how he may feel about them. He can be equal in his duties, but not necessarily equal in how he feels about them, and that is okay. It is up to you to decide if it's okay with *you* that one of your husband's wives has his heart more than you do. Or if you happened to be the wife that has his heart, how would you handle the jealousy coming from the other wife? And would you be able to contain your jealousy if the other wife is the favorite?

There are a few ideas out there on how to create a sense of equality and fairness among multiple wives. A fellow by the name of Dr. Umar Johnson suggested that if a man wants to marry multiple wives, he should marry women who are each on a different "list". The "A-list" would be the highest quality women, meaning she's a virgin or only been with one or two men, moral, no baggage and came from a good background. The "B-list" would be women that have a little baggage, been with a few men, background may not be perfect, but they are still good women. The "C-list" would be women that have a couple of kids, some emotional baggage, but not damaged beyond repair. And the "D-list" would mean you need to do a lot of praying and fasting in order to deal with her. Nonetheless, this type of system gives each polygynous man the opportunity to have an A-list wife, but also gives women who aren't A-list the opportunity to have a husband. It's a cool idea because it benefits both the polygynous men *and* the women.

But there are two issues with this system. One, if a man has an A-list and C-list wife, how's he going to keep the C-list wife from becoming jealous of the A-list wife? And two, if a woman is A-list, is it fair that she has to share her husband with a woman who's C-list? These are good questions, but there aren't many scriptures on how to address these issues. We do, however, see in scripture that the best way to reduce the chances of conflict is by separation (Genesis 13:7-9), so it would be safe to say that giving wives their own separate space would reduce chances of jealousy, envy and strife. They wouldn't have to be around each other all the time and wouldn't have to witness any favoritism, if there is any. Another way to help prevent jealousy (going back to Dr. Umar Johnson's system) is to marry women who are all on the same list or only one list apart. For example, a man would be better off marrying two A-list women or an A and B-list woman, rather than an A and C-list woman. The closer the women are in rank, the better the chances they will relate to one another instead of being jealous of each another.

Just like we cannot do much to stop a husband from having a favorite wife, they cannot do much to stop us from being jealous each other. However, wives *can* show each other dutiful love by treating each other respectfully and cordially. It's important that we discuss this, because there are men who promote polygyny that not only want women to share them with other women, but also want the women to be like sisters. As wonderful as that sounds, it is very idealistic. A man is lucky if he finds women that agree to polygyny at all, let alone agree to polygyny *and* develop a sisterhood with the other wives. That's hard to find, and if that's what polygynous men are requiring, they may miss out on the opportunity to practice the lifestyle. There is a lot of pressure on the wives to be perfect—they have to share a husband, share a home, get along with each other, be as close as sisters, and have no jealousy. This is not impossible, but it is a tall order. Even in scripture, we do not see such close bonds between women who were sharing a husband, even in cases when it was the wife's idea for her husband to take another wife. We'll discuss that in a brief moment.

Your husband's other wives are just that—*his other wives*. These women are not *your* wives, so they do not have to be your favorite people. However, if you establish a strong sisterhood with them, then that would make the experience of being in a polygynous marriage that much greater. Some women prefer to be in a polygynous marriage because they crave the love and support of other women. And then there are some women who prefer to have their own space and privacy without the other wives involved. They may crave love and support also, but prefer their friendship with women and marriage to be separate relationships that don't mix.

For instance, we don't know what kind of relationship Rachel and Leah had before they married Jacob, but we do know they became rivals after the fact. (Genesis 30:1) It's possible that they had a normal sisterly relationship beforehand. But after they were forced to share a husband, it brought out jealousy and envy. The same occurred with Sarah and Hagar in Genesis 16:3-4. Sharing a husband with another woman doesn't always bring out sisterly love, but rivalry instead. It sometimes causes women who may have been friends under other circumstances to become at odds with each other. The truth is it's okay to have a sisterhood with the other wives, and it's also okay *not* to. Neither is a sin. The problem comes in when the wives are forced to be in the opposite scenario that they desire. So, for your sake, make it known to your potential husband what you prefer and let him decide how he's going to manage everything.

The Head Wife

Sarah, Abraham's wife, would be considered as the "head wife" by modern day polygynists. A "head wife" is typically the first wife. She assists her husband in choosing, training and keeping the other wives orderly, which could be very helpful depending upon how many wives a man has. Let's say he has three. It would be nice to have someone help keep all those wives in order. If he is looking to add another wife to his family, it could help to have the input of the head wife to help him choose the woman that is best for them. But how would his other wives feel about one of them being the head wife? Wouldn't that be a form of favoritism? And would the head wife be reasonable in choosing wives for her husband? Furthermore, is this idea of a head wife supported in scripture?

It's safe to say that Sarah would be considered the head wife since she was the first wife, she suggested polygyny to her husband, she chose the second wife for him, and when conflict arose between her and his second wife, she was the one who handled it. Many women would love to have the same power and control that Sarah had in her marriage. But the intentions of the head wife is not always pure, and they are not always respectful of the other women. When Sarah told Abraham to marry her handmaiden, Hagar, it wasn't because she thought Hagar would make a great addition to her family. It wasn't because she was showing sisterly love. It was because she was impatient, old and unable to bare children of her own, so she suggested Abraham impregnate Hagar.

After Sarah finally bore her own son, she told Abraham to put his son, Ishmael and his mother Hagar, out of the house for good. (Genesis 21:10-13) Sarah had power and she definitely used it. Everything was orchestrated and controlled by her. We can definitely see why women would want to be in her position, but what woman would want to be in Hagar's position? Before you marry a polygynous man, make sure you find out what he thinks about having a head wife. You then must ask yourself if you are okay with being under the authority of another woman in your marriage. If that is okay with you, then proceed with your courtship, but do so with caution.

Just an FYI, the bible does not say that wives have authority over other wives. It is the husband that has authority over the wives. Ephesians 5:22-23 says, *"Wives, submit yourselves unto your own husbands as unto the Lord, for the husband is the head of the wife, even as Christ is the head of the church."* And 1 Corinthians 11:3 says, *"But I will have you know that the head of every man is Christ; and the head of the woman is the man; and the head of Christ is God."* Your husband should not put you in a position to submit yourself to his other wife while he sits back and lets her control you and the relationship. He is not treating you as a wife if he does that.

Whether a man has a head wife or not, naturally he may want his wives input on a woman before he makes her a wife, also. Some say that the wives should be the ones to choose the others. It *is* a good idea for the wives to have a say, but the final say should be the husband's. We talked about the purpose of marriage in the first chapter, and how the nation and its identity is formed through the father. Biblical nation building is patriarchal and it must continue to be that way if we want strong, healthy families. The problem with the wives choosing the other wives is that they may choose women who are more compatible with *them,* but incompatible with their husband. If Abraham would have chosen his own second wife instead of Sarah, it's possible he wouldn't have chosen Hagar. He probably would have chosen someone that he truly loves and cares for. Someone that could have become a lifelong partner to him. The mess that happened between Hagar and Sarah may not have went down if Abraham was running the show. These are all assumptions, of course. We don't know what would have happened, but the point is when men are in control, results are different than when women are in control.

Sidechick Shenanigans

There's a fine line between a second wife and a "sidechick" (or mistress). One is easily mistaken for the other because both of them are dating a married man. The differences between the two are not clear, so we must clear it up right now so that you won't be in jeopardy of being a mistress when you are really looking to be a wife. If you find yourself doing *any* of the things listed below, cease immediately. And if you are a wife and you suspect that the woman your husband is courting is doing any of these things, bring it to his attention ASAP.

1. **Sidechicks are secretive.** She does not tell or show her man her true intentions and she prefers to not meet or speak to his other women.

2. **Sidechicks are deceptive.** She may tell the wife (or suggest that the man tell his wife) that she is "just a friend" when in reality she is being courted for something more.

3. **Sidechicks pretend to polygynous.** She claims she is okay with polygyny, but her real intentions are to be with the man without other women in the picture. She always seems to disapprove every time he wants to court someone else.

4. **Sidechicks are selfish.** She has her own agenda, and if her man doesn't go along with it, she will do something to hurt him—either emotionally,

financially or physically. She does not care about the mission of the family—only what *she* wants out of the deal.

5. **Sidechicks are disorderly.** She lacks respect, manners and discipline. She does whatever she wants with no regard for how it will look or affect others. This is purposely done to cause chaos. If she acts out, she can intimidate her partner and be able to control the relationship.

Interestingly enough, some wives are guilty of these sidechick shenanigans, as well. They try to block their husband from taking on other wives, even if the other wife is compatible with him. They get jealous, and get cold feet. They agree to polygyny, but once their husband starts searching for other wives, they second guess if they want to share their husband. All of that is understandable, but still not acceptable. Polygyny may not be 100% comfortable for you all the time, but it isn't for your husband, either. The whole process is challenging for everyone, which is why it's best for everyone to show each other patience, understanding, and keep open communication so there is no confusion or deception going on.

NATION BUILDING
FOR WOMEN

CHAPTER 3

Joining His Nation

Benefits of Polygyny

The goal of a polygynous marriage is to create an upstanding nation that benefits all who are in it. There are so many benefits that we don't have time to cover, but let's start the basics...

Polygyny protects women and children. In societies where many of the women outnumber the men, polygyny makes it possible for them to have husbands and fathers for their children. It's interesting that no matter how bad of a predicament a woman is in, her goal is still to find a *monogamous* man even if she already has children with *other men*. This puts extra pressure on a monogamous man to take care of her and her children, which he may not be willing, ready or able to do. But in a polygynous setting, each adult can pool their resources to take care of the family, and the women can be of great help to each other in caring for the children.

Polygyny helps a man build his empire much quicker. I always say that if a man doesn't need help with his vision, then his vision isn't big enough. Having a help meet makes it possible for a man to build his empire bigger and faster, but imagine how much progress can be made if he had *multiple* help meets. That would be a game changer, especially for men in impoverished societies. If they had multiple wives, they could build their way out of poverty and stabilize themselves three times as fast.

Polygyny creates generational wealth. In a polygynous marriage, your ability to build enough wealth to leave behind for your children skyrockets. Nation building is very similar to building a business. You need a vision, a mission, a plan, and a team to carry it out. If, for example, your husband wants to start a business, you and his wives could be his team, and when your children are old enough, they can get involved in the business, as well. This way you all could keep the bulk of your wealth within your family instead of having to pay outsiders to do the work.

Polygyny creates a strong support system for wives. Think about how beneficial it would be to have someone to help you out with your household and childcare responsibilities *free of charge*! Think about how great it would be if you had someone to give you emotional and spiritual support when things get overwhelming. It can be very difficult for some women to develop a bond with their husband's other wives, but if you understood how greatly it could benefit all of you, you would probably make a sincere effort to become close. If you all are contributing to the upkeep and uprise of the same nation, that alone is a reason to get on the same page with one another.

Polygyny keeps the husband sexually fulfilled. Bet you weren't expecting this one to be listed, didn't you? But seriously, who wants to live with a grouchy husband who's mad at the world because he doesn't get enough sex? Sex doesn't just provide pleasure to a man, but also stress relief and mental clarity. If he's doing the oftentimes stressful job of building an empire, he's going to need as much "stress relief" as he can possibly get. If it bothers you that your husband will be having sex with his other wives, then you have to understand that it is just as important for your husband to be intimate with them as it is with you. It would not be right for him to deprive any of his wives of intimacy.

Polygyny keeps each wife on point. When a man only has one wife, she may not put much effort into her wifely duties because she knows she's all he has. But when there are multiple wives in the picture, she will step her game up because there is someone to compare her to. This is *healthy* competition. Wives are not to compete in the sense of trying to make the others look incompetent, but each wife is supposed to be the best she can be. However, some women just do not feel motivated to be their best *unless* they have competition. I hate to use the word "competition" because it suggests that someone will be the winner and another the loser, but healthy competition is good and will keep each woman striving to be her best.

Polygyny protects wives from infidelity. When a man has multiple wives, he probably won't get as bored with his wives as monogamous men get with theirs. Monogamists marry who they believe to be their one and only soul mate, then after a while, they get bored with her and begin to seek variety and excitement elsewhere. It's men's desire for variety that women mistake for *lust*. It isn't lust, but if men don't address this desire the proper way, it can *turn* to lust, and then infidelity. But if men have variety within their marriage, they have no need to go outside and seek it elsewhere.

Polygyny gives wives significance. A polygynous man should make it clear to his wives what role they will play in the family. If he doesn't acknowledge or appreciate each wife's unique talents and capabilities, then none of them will understand why they are even there. Why choose to be with them if there is nothing about them that is significant to the success of the family? But when the husband gives his wives a role, they feel like they are serving a real purpose, and not just there for their husband's amusement.

Polygyny teaches children how to work as a group. Children learn how family, unity and group economics works in a polygynous family. Personally, this is my absolute favorite thing about polygyny, because I didn't learn much about how to work with my family when I was growing up. Children in polygynous families get to see what a strong head of household looks like, what true sisterhood looks like, and how to work together to do business and generate wealth. Imagine the advantage that a young adult would have in the world if they came from a household where they learned these things firsthand. It's a priceless experience.

The Six Month Plan

If you're open to polygyny, then there are firm standards you must have in place in order to protect yourself. You don't want to be misled, have your time wasted or feelings played with, so it is best that you gather as much information as possible about the man, his spiritual life, his family plans and career path within a 6 month period. And don't be shy about holding him at a high standard, because he *should* be if he is trying to be the head of multiple women. Ephesians 5:25-29 says, *"Husbands, love your wives even as Christ loved the church and gave himself up for it, that he might sanctify and cleanse it with the washing of the water by the word, that he might present it to himself a glorious church not having spot, or* wrinkle or any such thing but that it should be holy and without blemish. So ought men to love their wives as their own bodies. He that loveth his wife loveth himself. For no man ever yet hated his own flesh, but nourisheth and cherisheth it even as the Lord the church:" This is what a polygynous man should be expected to do for all his wives to the best of his ability.

These are huge responsibilities and shouldn't be taken lightly by him nor his wife. A wife is symbolic of the church, and multiple wives are still yet symbolic of the church, which means a man who has multiple wives has an even greater responsibility. He cannot take on three wives, love one of them, leave the other two neglected and think that he has fulfilled his scriptural duty as a husband. It isn't fair to the wives who are unloved, because those women could've been with men who actually care about them.

To reduce your chances of ending up with a man who will mishandle your or his responsibilities, utilize the six month courtship plan below. It will save lots of time and make it possible for you to leave the situation earlier if it isn't working for you. Keep in mind that every man has his own way of courting, which will likely be different from the six month plan. However, you should still use this to your benefit because it will help you get the information you need to make a proper decision. The man's main focus is to see if you are the right fit for him. It is *your* responsibility to make sure *he* is a right fit for *you*. Don't let his vetting process distract you from finding out what you need to know about him

Month 1: Get to know his spiritual life. Your potential husband should be spiritually qualified to teach and lead you closer to God, and your spiritual discernment, faith and works should become greater under his leadership. A woman can be virtuous on her own, but it is the covering of a righteous husband that makes a woman's virtue increase to the max. You should spend at least a full month getting to know your potential husband spiritually, talking about God, scripture, prayer and how he plans to lead his family on a righteous path to God. You should also share with him how you would like him to enhance your spiritual life.

Month 2: Get to know his purpose. You need to know what your potential husband feels God has called him to do in life. He should know his purpose and already walking in it. If he has not already gotten started on doing what he feels God has called him to do, then he doesn't need to get a wife yet. He needs to get started on his mission first. Remember: The mission isn't a part of his marriage, the marriage is a part of his mission. The marriage is secondary to his relationship with God, so whatever God called him to do, he should be doing that when you meet him, not waiting on you to be his wife so he can get started. Question him to see how passionate and ambitious he is, and check to see if what he is doing is fruitful. This helps you to know if he has the ability to provide for you or not.

Month 3: Get to know his expectations. You will need to know what your potential husband expects from you. Since you may be his *help meet,* you have to come to the table with your own passions, skills and abilities. Be prepared to share these things with him. He should ask, but if he doesn't, go ahead and volunteer the information and pay attention to his reaction. If he asks you what you have to offer, don't take offense. He has every right to question you to see if you have the ability to add something to the nation that he's building. A man who is serious about making you a wife will be serious about making sure you're qualified. During month 2, you should also ask him periodically if he needs you to do something for him. If he always answers no, that is a red flag. If he doesn't have anything for you to do, then he doesn't really need a help meet.

Month 4: Get to know his family values. During the fourth month, the two of you should be taking time to compare and contrast your family values. You need to know how many wives and children he wants, how he wants his children to be parented and how he wants to be treated by his wives. And of course, you need to know how he intends on leading you and his wives. What is his definition of manhood and leadership? What is his definition of love and protection? He should also tell you what role he wants you to play in his family. Some men want their wives to join each other in household chores and responsibilities, others may have different ideas, so get to know what he expects, that way you can decide if you are capable of fulfilling those expectations or not.

Month 5: Get to know his wife. If you get to this point, then that means the first four months were successful for both you and your potential husband. That is great. Now you need to meet his current wife/wives to feel them out and get to know a little about each other. Your potential husband should have already told them about you at this point, so there shouldn't be any surprises. Sometimes the wife doesn't want her to have another wife, so if you are not welcomed, you need to know that. Now, just because you aren't welcomed by the other wife, doesn't mean you have to leave. But be aware that if you continue your relationship with him, the other wife will most likely do all she can to make you go away.

Take Jacob's wives Rachel and Leah, for example. Although they were blood sisters, the two of them were constantly competing and taunting each other because they did not want to share Jacob. They both felt entitled to him. Rachel felt entitled because she is who he originally wanted to marry, and Leah felt entitled because she was the oldest, and it was a cultural practice that the oldest marries first. If Jacob could have kept these women separated, maybe things would have went a lot smoother. Maybe you should make sure separation is an option for your protection. Don't let a man make you live with a wife that doesn't want you there.

In any case, when meeting the wife, ask her whatever you want to know about her, their home life, and what she expects from a "sister wife" (we'll talk more about that later). This would be her opportunity to get to know you as well, and the two of you may develop a bond. Not that there has to be one, because that is not a scriptural requirement (we'll talk about this later, too). If the meeting with the wife goes well, it would be a good idea for the two of you to keep in touch.

Month 6: Get to know his financial expectations. Lastly, you need to know what his financial/economic expectations are for his family. Now is the time when he discloses his income, you disclose yours, and he discloses the financial state he wants his family to be in for the future. This information is kind of personal, but by this point, the both of you should be willing and ready to talk about these things if you are serious about marrying. He also needs to tell you how he expects you and his wives to contribute to the economic well-being of the family. Does he want you to work? Does he want you to have your own business? Does he want you to help him with *his*? Ask these questions and any others you can think of to get to know his financial expectations for his family.

This six month plan can help the both of you get important information in a timely fashion so no one's time is wasted. At any step along the way, you can end the courtship if you feel that he isn't the right fit for you. It helps, though, if you have a male overseer to help you make your decision. This could be any trusted male, preferably an older one, who has the wisdom to give you sound advice about your relationship. It would also be a good idea if the man who's courting you meets your overseer within the six month period. You will want as much guidance and protection throughout this process as you can get. A polygynous lifestyle was not easy to practice back in biblical times so it is especially challenging now.

If your courtship is long distance, the man should still plan to meet with you within 6 months. But if you feel you need a little more time, then please take all the time you need. This plan is just a suggestion to help the both of you make significant progress in a reasonable amount of time without either of you having the space to play games with each other. Polygyny is serious business and it should be handled as such. The more time it takes, the more likely it is that you aren't compatible.

The Good Wife

No matter how many wives your husband has, it should be your goal to be the best wife to him as you can be. Polygyny can actually make you a better wife because having *healthy* competition gives you a reason to want to put in more effort. Women in monogamous marriages sometimes get complacent because no one is keeping them on their toes. There is no pressure on them to improve in any way. But in polygyny, the women know the other wives bring something of value to the table, and they do not want to be the only one who doesn't.

When all the wives bring their A-game, the whole family benefits. They feel more secure in their marriage, the man feels satisfied with his choices in wives, and the wives display a great example of what a dedicated wife looks like to their children. Understand that not all competition is mean spirited. There is such thing as friendly competition, and women need to learn to engage in it more. We don't have to be nasty or tear each other down to compete, all we have to do is use each other's greatness as motivation to do better ourselves. Competition is not the only thing that makes you a better wife, but the characteristics listed below can, as well. The bible calls these "the fruit of the spirit". Galatians 5:22 says, *"But the fruit of the spirit is love, joy, peace, longsuffering, gentleness, goodness, faith, meekness, temperance: against such, there is no law"*...

Love. You should have a loving heart, not just for the sake of your husband, but for the sake of the women that you will share your husband with. Show them the love that you would like to receive. There may even be times when you will have to correct them, but do that out of love, too.

Joy. To have joy doesn't mean to never feel sad, disappointed or angry at times. It just means that you are generally happy in spirit, even if you technically don't feel happy all the time. Bring the spirit of joy into your marriage. Your whole household will benefit.

Peace. You will need to be mentally and spiritually sound if you are entering into a polygynous marriage. Do not bring in a spirit of unrest because it is contagious. If one of the wives is unpeaceful, it disturbs the other wives and causes confusion.

Longsuffering (patience). A lot of couples have ended up in divorce because they couldn't manage the ups and downs of their marriage. I'm sure you don't want to end up this way, so you, your husband and your sisters will need a healthy amount of patience in order to make your polygynous marriage work.

Gentleness. A woman with a gentle spirit is considerate about how she addresses and approaches others. This is a helpful way to be, especially while dealing with your fellow sisters. It reduces the chances of conflict escalating between you.

Goodness. You can't build a nation of good people if you lack goodness yourself. Your good morals will be instilled in your children, but if you lack morality, you will be instilling that in them, too.

Faith. Matthew 17:20 says, *"Verily I say unto you, if ye have faith as a grain of mustard seed, ye shall say unto the mountain, "Remove hence to yonder place, and it shall remove. And nothing shall be impossible unto you."* Isn't that powerful? A woman who has faith has that same type of power.

Meekness. If you're not a meek, or humble woman, polygyny will be a very bumpy ride for you. A meek and humble woman brings peace to her marriage and those around her, including her sisters. As Psalm 37:11 says, *"But the meek shall inherit the earth and shall delight themselves in the abundance of peace."*

Temperance. A disciplined woman is a very valuable woman for a man to have on his team. The more disciplined you are, and the more you teach it to your children, the more successful you can help your husband's nation to become.

A woman fit for a polygynous marriage is a special kind of woman. If you know any women who are already involved in a successful polygynous marriage, you can probably see for yourself that they have many, if not all, of these character traits. We all would like to think we possess the fruit of the spirit, but when we find ourselves in challenging situations, it brings out who we really are. I encourage you to develop the fruit of the spirit because you *will* need them, even if you decide to marry monogamously.

The Exit Plan

We're almost done, but we can't close out until we discuss one last thing—*leaving* a polygynous marriage. Marriage is supposed to be a lifetime, but it has become way too easy to just leave. Leaving should only be an option in extreme cases where you are left no choice. If you feel there is something going on in your marriage that is unbearable to you, first give your husband and/or sister wives time to correct it. And if it not corrected, then hopefully you will only decide to leave for a *lawful* reason. Make sure you are able to leave safely and securely. Before and during your marriage, make frequent contributions to your own emergency bank account (each wife should have one) just in case an unexpected expense arises. No woman should marry without any idea of what she will do or where she will go in the event of divorce. Heck, she may not even be the one to leave *him—he* may decide to divorce *her*, or he may die and leave her and the children behind. Either way, every woman should know what she would do if this were to happen. You should also have some type of legal right/documentation that protects you and your children if the worst case scenario was to occur. Is your name on the bank accounts and property? Are you in his will? Do you have power of attorney? Each wife should have legal rights of some kind. If a man does not want you to have these rights, then he is not to be trusted.

Whether you decide that polygyny is right for you or not, I hope *Nation Building for Women* made it easier for you to go forward with your eyes wide open. I pray that your questions were answered and you are more enlightened about the practice, whether you want it for yourself or not. I'm sure you still have questions or opinions about polygyny that weren't addressed in this book, but those questions could be better answered by men and women who have been in successful polygynous marriages for years. This book is just designed to properly prepare you for courting a polygynous man in case you decide to go that route. If not, you still have a wealth of knowledge that can help you before entering a courtship with *anyone*. It's always best to be armed with knowledge, and I pray *Nation Building for Women* succeeded in assisting with that. God bless.

NATION BUILDING
FOR MEN

a little word of advice for
Polygynous Men

In the earlier edition of *Nation Building For Women*, this particular section was not in the book, but I thought it was necessary to add it to the revised version. After the early edition was released, I got so many questions from men even though the book was for women! I was pleasantly surprised by how many men read it. So, if you are a man reading this right now, I first want to say that it is very commendable that you are a polygynist, even if you haven't officially began practicing it. Being willing to take on multiple wives is a huge responsibility, plus, you are providing a great service to women by giving more of us a chance to be married. Women tend to favor monogamy because it is exclusive, but its exclusivity is what hurts us. It's good for the women who are chosen, but bad for the many women who are not.

Of course, I'm a woman, so I am only speaking on what I perceive to be the most significant benefits of polygyny for *us*, but there is lots in it for you, too. I'm sure there are men who can better inform you on those benefits. What I would like to do is give you a little advice on how to deal with the women that you are courting for marriage. None of this is set in stone, but this is just a little cheat sheet on how to make the process of courting and vetting wives easier for you.

1. **Never tell any woman that you are single.** Even if you really *are* single, never tell the woman that you are interested in that you are not currently courting anyone else. When a woman thinks she is the only woman, she will get comfortable with it and want it to stay that way. Then when you try to bring another woman into the picture, she will say, *"We're already happy as we are. Why can't we just keep things the way it is?"* I would even suggest that when you marry, don't take a long time to start courting another wife, because married women get very comfortable with monogamy after a time, too. Before you know it, your wife will be asking you not to marry again, even though you told her upfront you were a polygynist. Never let any woman get too comfortable with monogamy if polygyny is the goal.

2. **Be very careful of who your first wife is.** Who your first wife is can make or break your polygynist experience. The first wife pretty much sets a standard for the others. If she is loving, submissive, and helpful, then the other wives will know they must be that way to harmonize with your family. But if she is rebellious, mean and jealous, then the other wives will feel like it is acceptable for them to be that way, also. It may even cause a good woman to not want to be with you because she doesn't want to deal with your hateful wife. Make sure your first wife sets a great example of womanhood and sisterhood so that the other women who come in may know that they must at least measure up to what you already have.

3. **Don't let a woman talk you into monogamy if that isn't what you want.** Some
   of you may attempt to practice polygyny but find that it makes more sense
   for you to just be monogamous. Others may be monogamous but find that
   it makes more sense to be polygynous. Understand that most *women* think
   monogamy makes more sense, and that you only want to be polygynous
   just for kicks. They view it as something you don't *really* need to do, and they
   may question why don't you just settle for monogamy and call it a day. If
   polygyny is what you want, then you have to stand your ground and never
   give any indication that you will settle for anything else. As long as a woman
   thinks that you are willing to compromise on this, she will definitely try to get
   you to compromise.

4. **Inform your wife when you are courting another woman.** If your wife is
   humble enough to agree to polygyny, then should at least show her the
   courtesy of informing her when you've found a lady that you are interested
   in. You don't have to introduce the two of them just yet, but simply letting
   her know that you found someone you like gives her time to start preparing
   herself to meet her and possibly be her sister wife. There are men who court
   the other woman for quite some time, and then suddenly spring it on their
   wife that they found a candidate for a second wife. The wife had no time to
   mentally prepare for the transition into polygyny. Always be sure to make
   your wife aware that there is another woman you are seeing so that she can
   prepare herself in advance.

5. **Understand that a lot of women have been traumatized by infidelity.** To
   them, polygyny reminds them of being cheated on, and although the
   women in polygynous relationships consented to being there, those who do
   not understand it still view it as a form of cheating. The only way to ensure
   that your wives don't feel this way is to have them consent to polygyny first.
   Biblically you have the right to have another wife whether your previous

wives approve or not, but out of consideration, try not to do that. Try not to force polygyny on any woman that did not agree to it.

6. **If she agrees to polygyny, but changes her mind after marriage, then proceed with polygyny anyway.** I've had many men ask me what should they do if their wife agrees to polygyny, but later changes her mind. If she doesn't want it anymore, yet she doesn't leave, then she is simply trying to get you to bend to her will. I advise that you proceed with polygyny despite her wishes. The "bait and switch" is a manipulation tactic that women use because it *works*. Usually after a man is married to you, it is easier to get him to do whatever you want because you're his wife now. Women know this and that is why they wait until after they're married to switch up on you. As the head of household, you must always remain in control of how your household will be ran, and if you said that polygyny was going to be practiced, then you must stick with that even when your wife tries to get you to change your mind. If she can convince you to change your mind on matters such as this, then *she* is the head of the household.

7. **Issues between you and your first wife should be fixed before taking another wife.** As I mentioned earlier, your first wife sets a standard for the other wives, and if you're are at odds, it will make it difficult for the other wives to harmonize with your family. If for some reason you cannot get your first wife under control, then you will have to find a way to ensure your second wife that those issues will not spill into your marriage with *her*. The best way to do that is by keeping the two marriages completely separate.

8. **If all you want are maids and nannies, then get maids and nannies.** When a woman marries, she is expecting to be a wife, not only a servant. Nothing wrong with being a servant, but do not lead your future wives into believing that they are going to have a relationship with you if all they'll be doing is

helping you and/or your wife around the house. There are men who get a second wife for these purposes only, and then the second wife ends up feeling used because she is treated more like a handmaiden than a wife. Again, if all you really need are handmaidens, then you are well within your right to have them. Just do not lead them to believe they will be wives.

9. **Give your potential wives small tasks to complete to test their submission.** There is no way that you will know that a woman can submit or follow instructions unless you actually give her instructions to follow. Ask her to do small tasks for you while you are courting and notice her reaction. Does she act as if you don't have the right to ask her to do anything, or does she willingly oblige? If she voluntarily asks *you* if there's anything she can help you with, this is a very good sign.

10. **Get a woman who's willing to help you find your other wives.** Notice I said *help* find the other wives, not that they should be responsible for finding them on their own. When a woman is willing to help you, she is showing you that she is in alignment with your plan. However, if she insists on finding them without your help, then that indicates that she wants to have most of the control over who is chosen. Your wives are *your* wives, and you should have the most input on whether or not someone will be courted. Your wife is only there to assist.

11. **Don't have a revolving door of women.** If you take yourself seriously and you want women to take you seriously too, then you cannot have a revolving door of women coming in and out of your life. It will soon look like you are just having fun, and it's possible your wife will lose respect for you *and* polygyny if she sees you practicing it in an indecent way. Be a good example of a polygynist. Many men and women do not know how polygyny

should be practiced, so be one who takes polygyny seriously enough to represent it with class.

12.   **Last, but not least, be a good husband to your wives, no matter how many you have.** Your wives don't just want to be married, but they also want a *husband.* As simple as this may sound, I personally do not think that some polygynist men understand that every woman wants a certain experience after she is married. She does not want to feel like her marriage life is no better than being single. She doesn't want to feel lonely, and she doesn't want to feel like she doesn't get enough time, attention, support or affection from her husband. As a polygynist man, it is on you to make sure all your wives get what they need. If you have any feeling that you can't give a woman what she needs, let her go find someone who can. Don't take her as a wife, then let her go without her needs being fulfilled.

If you would like to read more about this topic, please check out the second edition of *Nation Building For Women: Exposing the Destructive Nature of Monogamy.* I wish you all the best on your future polygynous marriage. May you find the loves of your life that you are looking for. If it is God's will that you have them, then show him glory by treating your wives as he would want you to treat them. Thank you for supporting Queens of Virtue Marriage Prep & Femininity Coaching. God bless.

...more
resources from

Queens of Virtue

marriage
prep &
femininity
coaching

Queens of Virtue Marriage Prep & Femininity Coaching provides biblical based coaching to women of all ages on how to get in touch with their feminine nature. This service is mainly geared toward single women, as it is designed to help them prepare for marriage. However, many single *and* married women across the country and abroad have benefited from Queens of Virtue coaching, whether it was through one-on-one sessions, books, or free social media content.

If you would like to request a coaching session or enroll in a course with Queens of Virtue, you can do so by emailing pinkhouseenterprises@gmail.com. Please keep in mind that sessions and courses are not free (see prices below), but we do not charge if a client only has a quick question or two. We are first and foremost here to help.

Each Queens of Virtue Coaching Session is $75 for 2 hours. You have the option of doing the full 2 hours at one time or dividing it into two 1 hour sessions. You can schedule your sessions via phone, video chat, or DM. During your session, you are allowed to ask whatever questions you want. If you don't have any specific questions, just let us know what your concerns are upfront at the time of payment, and we will create a custom lesson just for you. *There is no additional charge for this.

The price of each Queens of Virtue Course is $750 for 3 months. At the end of each week, there will be a 2 hour follow up session to review the information you studied and to answer any questions you may have. Once your course is completed, you won't only leave with a wealth of knowledge and a new state of mind, but you will receive an amazing gift exclusively for Queens of Virtue clients.

There are four courses to choose from: The *Bride to Be* Course, which is for single women who want to train to become suitable wives, and married women who want to sharpen their wifely skills. *The Hyper Femininity* Course is for women who are trying to overcome the effects of feminism and get in touch with their feminine nature. *The Nation Building For Women* Course is for women who are exploring polygyny and want to prepare to be a sister wife, as well as learn the proper ways of dealing with a polygynous man. And finally, *The Hypergamous Femininity* Course is for women who are dating or want to date men who are wealthy, affluent and/or public figures. This course teaches how to gain access to, and become a potential wife, for high caliber men.

Your course packages will be delivered to you by mail. Some items may be delivered digitally. Included in each course package is...

- 12 Customized Weekly Curriculums, designed specifically for your unique concerns
- 36 Assignments (3 per week), some assignments will need to be turned in
- 2 Hour Weekly Sessions, for questions and reviews
- 3 Queens of Virtue books, for studying and reviewing
- Feminine Fashion Guide (video), to assist you in polishing your look
- Feminine Makeup Class (video), to assist you in polishing your look
- Money Class DVD by Suze Orman, for financial literacy, assignments will also be associated with this
- Home Décor book, some assignments will be associated with this book
- Cookbook, some assignments will be associated with this book
- Expense Tracker
- Calculator
- Notebook/Journal/Pens
- Bible, because we all need one ☺

If you are interested in enrolling in a Queens of Virtue Course or Coaching Session, please contact us at pinkhouseenterprises@gmail.com. You can also message us on Facebook (Queens of Virtue) or Instagram (@hyper_femininity), and we'll be glad to get you started.

Made in United States
North Haven, CT
30 September 2022

24692592R00024